THE PURR-FECT SCIENCE FAIR
Workbook

5 Experiments You Can Test, Measure, and Explain

By Amy Bae

A Bae Data Lab INC Book

Written by Amy Bae
Illustration direction and concept by Amy Bae; visuals developed through generative design techniques and extensively edited by hand.

Published by Bae Data Lab INC

ISBN (Paperback): 978-1-968687-09-0

First edition, January 2026
Printed in the United States

Table of Contents

GETTING STARTED

Welcome, Junior Scientist!

Hi there! We're so glad you picked up this Science Fair Workbook to guide you through your very own experiment or investigation.

In this workbook, you'll take the lead as a young scientist, using curiosity, creativity, and careful observation to explore a question that interests you.

This book is your special space to:
- Plan your science fair project step by step.
- Record your observations and data.
- Learn how scientists think and work.
- Think like a real scientist, just like Adeline, Blue, and Oreo.

All you need is a curious mind, a few materials, and the courage to ask questions. Remember: every scientist starts by wondering "What if...?"

Science is about asking questions, testing ideas, and paying attention to what you discover. This workbook will help you organize your project, track your results, and communicate your findings so you can enter your science fair with confidence.

How to Use This Book

This book is made to help you complete your own science fair project. You can use it from start to finish or just the parts that help you the most.

Here is how it works:

- Plan Your Project: Write your science question, hypothesis, and materials.
- Do the Experiment: Follow the steps, take notes, and record what you see.
- Track Your Data: Use the data tables and graph pages to keep your results organized.
- Learn the Science: Read short fact pages that explain key science ideas and help you understand your experiment.
- Wrap It Up: Write your results, conclusion, and reflection.

This workbook can be used on its own or alongside The Purr-fect Science Fair Project book series. Each story in the series explores a different science topic and encourages kids to think, test, and discover, just like real scientists.

You'll also find helpful tips from Adeline and her two cats, Blue and Oreo, sprinkled throughout this guide to cheer you on and help you stay curious as you create your own experiment.

Project Board Pages

Some pages in this guide are marked with the special project board symbol.

These pages are designed to help you build each part of your science fair project board.

When you see the symbol:
- Pay extra attention to your notes.
- Write clearly and neatly.
- Think about how this information will look on your final board.

By the time you finish, you'll have everything you need to put together a strong and organized science fair display.

Plan It Out: Work Backward from the Science Fair

Every great project starts with a plan!
Now that you know how this workbook works, it's time to make a plan! Every great scientist and engineer starts with a timeline. Use this page to set your key milestones, mark important due dates, and make sure you have plenty of time to explore, test, and create before science fair day.

Key Milestones

Proposal due by _____

Testing begins _____

Data collection complete _____

Project board complete _____

Project due to school _____

My Science Fair Date: _____

Now fill in your timeline below to plan each step from finish to start.

Tips for Setting Your Target Dates

- Start with your science fair date.
- Count backward to plan when each part should be finished.
- Allow extra days for drying time, printing, or fixing mistakes.
- Add any teacher check-in or approval deadlines.
- Give yourself "buffer time" in case a test needs to be repeated.

🐾 Cat Tip: Check your timeline every few days. If you're ahead, great! If you're behind, adjust your plan so you stay on track.

My Science Fair Milestones

Milestone	Target Date	Suggestion
Science fair day		The big day to share my project.
Practice my presentation		Do this at least 2 days before the science fair. Practice with a friend or family member.
Put together project board		Start assembling your board about 5 days before the science fair. Add visuals, captions, charts, and photos.
Write up project board sections		Write your introduction, question, hypothesis, materials, procedure, results, and conclusion before gluing anything down.
Graphing complete		After you finish data collection. Create your bar, line, or pie charts and label everything clearly.
Data collection complete		When all tests or trials are done. Plan time afterward to analyze and organize your results.
Testing begins		Start early. Testing time depends on your experiment. Make room in your schedule for multiple trials.
Model or build complete (if needed)		Build your model or setup before testing. Test that it works correctly.
Proposal approved		Turn in your proposal early. Add any teacher check-in dates to your timeline.
Choose my topic and question		Do this at the very beginning. Pick a topic you can test and write a clear question.

Background

Before you begin your experiment, it helps to understand what you're testing and why it matters.

This section will help you build background knowledge, learn key science vocabulary, and explore the big ideas behind your project.

You'll learn:

- What your topic is about and why it's important
- How your question connects to the real world
- How scientists study and test ideas
- Why curiosity and observation are the starting points for discovery

As you read, use the "Words to Know" boxes and short activities to practice using science terms. Don't worry if a word feels new. Scientists learn by exploring, and you're one of them!

🐾 Oreo Says: "Every great scientist starts by learning the basics. Let's build your science vocabulary!"

🐾 Blue Adds: "And maybe discover a cozy spot for my next nap while you learn!"

What Is the Scientific Method?

The scientific method is a step-by-step way to explore questions about the world. Scientists ask questions, make predictions, test ideas, and share what they discover. You'll use these same steps as you plan and complete your own science fair project.

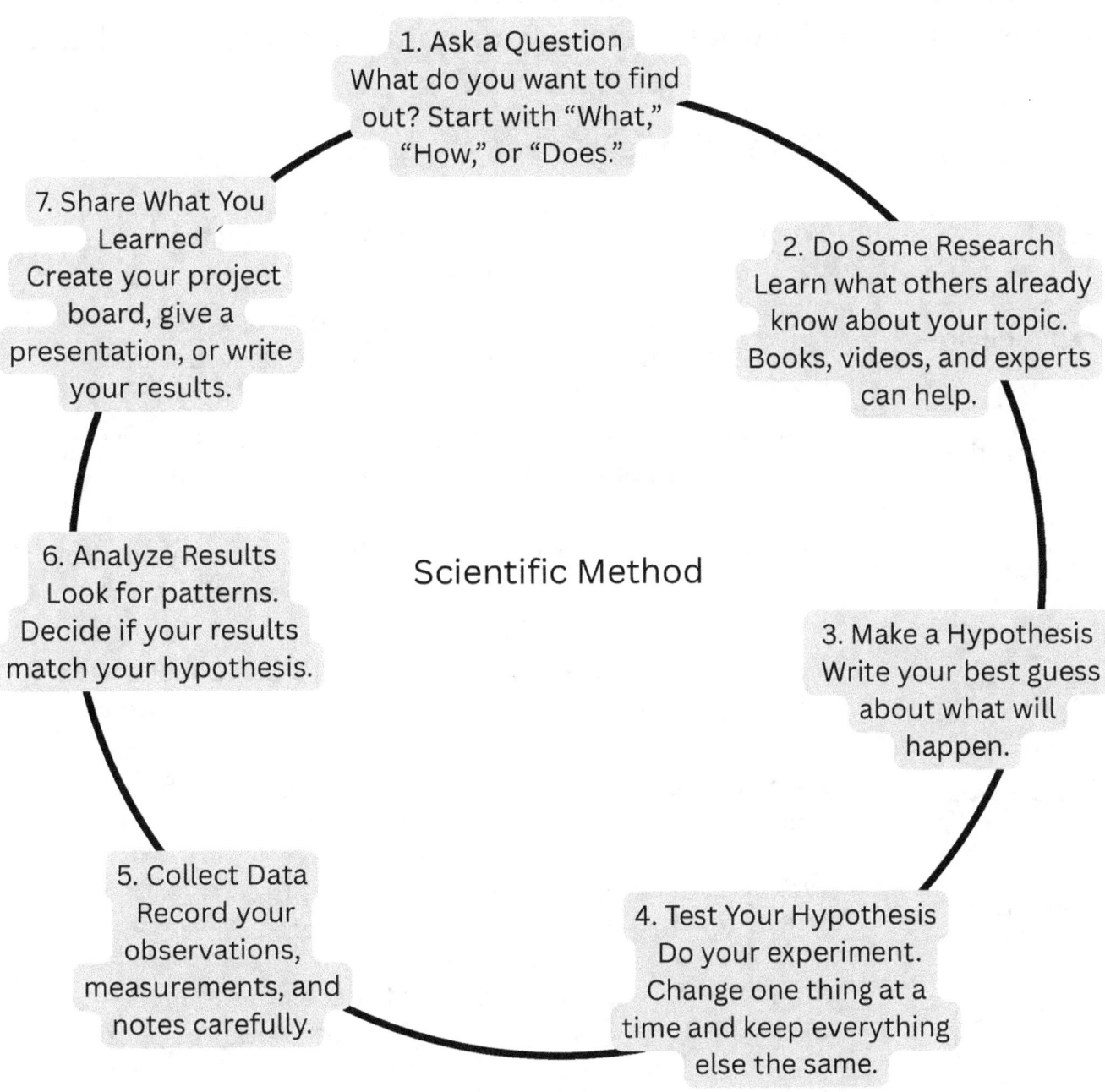

1. Ask a Question
What do you want to find out? Start with "What," "How," or "Does."

2. Do Some Research
Learn what others already know about your topic. Books, videos, and experts can help.

3. Make a Hypothesis
Write your best guess about what will happen.

4. Test Your Hypothesis
Do your experiment. Change one thing at a time and keep everything else the same.

5. Collect Data
Record your observations, measurements, and notes carefully.

6. Analyze Results
Look for patterns. Decide if your results match your hypothesis.

7. Share What You Learned
Create your project board, give a presentation, or write your results.

Scientific Method

WORDS TO KNOW

Every scientist uses special words to describe what they study. These science terms help you explain your ideas clearly and understand how your project connects to the real world.

As you work through your science fair project, write down any new words you learn. Try using them in your notes, data tables, and final presentation.

Here are a few to get you started:

Word	What It Means	Example or Picture
Experiment	A test or activity to learn something new.	I tested how different materials absorb water.
Observation	Using your senses to notice and record what happens.	I saw that the sugar dissolved faster in warm water.
Question	What you are trying to find out.	Which paper towel absorbs the most water?
Hypothesis	Your best guess about what will happen and why.	I think thicker paper towels will absorb more water.
Investigation	A way to explore and answer a question.	I compared three brands to find the best one.
Prediction	What you think will happen before you test it.	I predict Brand A will hold the most water.
Conclusion	What you learned after your experiment.	My data showed my hypothesis was correct.
Results	What happened in your experiment.	Brand A held 50 mL of water.

Word	What It Means	Example or Picture
Independent Variable	What you change on purpose.	The brand of paper towel.
Dependent Variable	What you measure or observe.	How much water each towel absorbed.
Controlled Variable	What stays the same in the experiment.	The amount of water used for each test.
Data	The information or measurements you collect.	I recorded each trial's result in a chart.
Bar Graph	Uses bars to compare amounts.	Shows how each towel performed.
Line Graph	Shows changes over time.	Tracks plant growth each day.
Pictograph	Uses pictures or symbols to show data.	Each drop stands for 10 mL of water.
X-Axis	The bottom line of a graph (what you measured).	Paper towel brand.
Y-Axis	The side line of a graph (how much).	Milliliters of water.
Label	A word or phrase that explains what something means.	"Water Absorbed" label on the Y-axis.
Title	The name of a graph or project.	"Which Paper Towel Holds the Most Water?"
Presentation	Sharing your work with others.	Explaining your project at the science fair.
Display Board	A board that shows your question, data, and results.	My poster showed photos, graphs, and my conclusion.

Safety First!

Before you begin your experiment, it's important to think about safety. Scientists always plan how to work carefully and protect themselves, others, and the environment.
Follow these safety tips to make sure your experiment is safe and successful.

General Safety Rules:

- Always ask an adult before starting your experiment.
- Read directions carefully before using materials.
- Wear goggles, gloves, or an apron if needed.
- Keep food and drinks away from your experiment area.
- Never taste or eat materials used in your project.
- Be gentle with living things like plants or animals.
- Wash your hands after finishing your experiment.
- Clean up your workspace and return materials safely.

Safety Planning:

Think about your own project. What might need extra care or supervision?

My Experiment Safety Plan:

Possible risks or safety concerns:_____

How I will stay safe:_____

Adult helper or supervisor: _____

🐾 Blue's Tip: "No running, no splashing, and no surprises."
🐾 Oreo Says: "Unless the surprise is tuna. Then I'm in."

5 SCIENCE FAIR EXPERIMENTS

Science Fair Experiments to Try!

Fun ideas to test, explore, and spark your next project!

Welcome to the experiment section of the book!
Here you'll find a collection of hands-on science fair projects you can try at home, in class, or anywhere curiosity strikes.

Each page gives you everything you need — the goal, materials, step-by-step directions, and a short explanation of the science behind it. These experiments match what you learned in the workbook about asking questions, planning fair tests, and making observations.

Use this section to:
- Try real science experiments on your own
- Get inspired for your next science fair project
- Practice collecting data and noticing patterns
- Discover how everyday materials can lead to amazing discoveries

You don't need to write in these pages. They're ready to use alongside your workbook or on their own whenever you feel like exploring.

🐾 Adeline says: "These are some of my favorite experiments to start with!"
🐾 Blue adds: "Follow the steps, take good notes, and have fun testing your ideas."
🐾 Oreo reminds you: "Keep the fur off the tape and the snacks out of the science!"

Land Ice vs. Sea Ice

Does melting ice always raise sea level?

Goal: Test how melting land ice and melting sea ice affect water levels differently.

You'll Need

- 4 ice cubes (equal size and weight)
- 2 bowls or containers
- Air dry clay (2 lumps of equal size)
- Water (equal amount for each model)
- Stopwatch or timer
- Paper and markers for recording observations

Steps

1. Roll the two lumps of clay into flat shapes and press one into the bottom of each container to form the "land."
2. Pour the same amount of water into both containers until it just covers the clay.
3. In the first container, place two ice cubes on top of the clay land to represent land ice.
4. In the second container, place two ice cubes floating on the water to represent sea ice.
5. Mark the starting water level on each container using a marker or a piece of tape.
6. Start your timer and observe as the ice melts.
7. Record your observations over time and note which container's water level rises more after the ice melts.

What's Happening

When sea ice melts, it doesn't raise sea level because it is already floating in the water. Land ice, however, sits on solid ground, so when it melts, it adds more water to the ocean. This experiment helps scientists understand how melting glaciers and ice sheets contribute to rising sea levels around the world.

The Lemon Battery
Can fruit make electricity?

Goal: Test if lemons can create enough electricity to power a small light or clock.

You'll Need
- 2–3 lemons
- 2 zinc nails (or galvanized nails)
- 2 copper pennies (or copper strips)
- 3 alligator clip wires
- 1 small LED light or digital clock
- A knife (ask an adult for help)

Steps
1. Roll the lemons gently on the table to loosen the juice inside.
2. Push one zinc nail and one copper penny into each lemon. Keep them about two inches apart and make sure they do not touch.
3. Use alligator clips to connect the zinc nail from one lemon to the copper penny in the next lemon.
4. Connect the remaining zinc and copper ends to the LED light or clock.
5. Watch what happens when the circuit is complete.
6. Try adding or removing lemons to see how it changes the brightness.

What's Happening
Lemons contain acid that helps electricity move between two different metals. The zinc and copper react with the lemon juice to create an electric current that travels through the wires. More lemons make more voltage, which makes the light shine brighter!

Snowy Crystals

Can you grow your own snowflake?

Goal: Create crystal "snowflakes" using simple materials to explore how real snow crystals form.

You'll Need

- 1 cup of hot water (ask an adult for help)
- 3 tablespoons of borax powder
- 1 wide-mouth glass jar or cup
- 1 pipe cleaner
- String
- Pencil or chopstick
- Spoon

Steps

1. Shape your pipe cleaner into a snowflake or star. Make sure it fits inside the jar without touching the sides.
2. Tie one end of the string to your snowflake and the other end to the pencil. Lay the pencil across the top of the jar so the snowflake hangs inside.
3. Pour 1 cup of hot water into the jar.
4. Stir in the borax, one tablespoon at a time, until it no longer dissolves (this means the solution is saturated).
5. Lower the snowflake into the jar and make sure it hangs freely.
6. Leave the jar undisturbed overnight.
7. The next day, lift out your snowflake and observe the crystals that formed!

What's Happening

As the water cools, borax particles stick together and attach to the pipe cleaner, forming crystals. This is similar to how real snowflakes form when water vapor in cold air freezes around tiny dust particles, creating beautiful crystal shapes.

Rainbow Volcano

What causes a volcanic eruption?

Goal: Create a model volcano to explore what happens when gases build up and escape during an eruption.

You'll Need

- 1 small bottle
- 2 tablespoons of baking soda
- Vinegar
- Dish soap
- Food coloring (any color or mix several)
- Glitter (optional)
- Air dry clay, modeling clay, or homemade dough (optional for volcano shape)
- Tray or surface cover

Steps

1. Place the bottle on a tray or protected surface.
2. (Optional) Use clay or dough to build a volcano shape around the bottle, leaving the top open for the eruption. Let it dry or set if needed.
3. Add 2 tablespoons of baking soda into the bottle.
4. Add a few drops of dish soap, food coloring, and glitter if you'd like some sparkle.
5. Slowly pour vinegar into the bottle and watch the colorful, foamy eruption!
6. Try changing the amount of vinegar or baking soda to see how it affects the size of the eruption.

What's Happening

When baking soda and vinegar mix, they create a chemical reaction that produces carbon dioxide gas. The bubbles of gas get trapped in the dish soap, forming foam that looks like lava flowing from a volcano.

Dissolving Candy Test

Which liquid dissolves candy fastest?

Goal: Compare how different liquids dissolve the same candy.

You'll Need

- 4 clear cups
- Water, vinegar, milk, and soda
- Same type of hard candy or coated candy
- Timer
- Spoon for gentle stir

Steps

1. Fill each cup with a different liquid.
2. Drop the same candy into each cup at the same time.
3. Start the timer and observe.
4. Gently stir each cup the same way every minute.
5. Record time to dissolve coating or full candy.
6. Compare results.

What's Happening

Acidity, temperature, and fat content affect dissolving speed. Some coatings dissolve faster in water or acid.

PLANNING YOUR PROJECT

The Proposal: Planning Your Science Fair Project

Before you begin your experiment, it's time to plan your project like a real scientist!

A proposal is a short plan that explains your science idea. It tells what question you want to answer, what you think will happen, and how you plan to test it.

Scientists write proposals to organize their ideas and make sure their tests are fair, safe, and clear. Most school science fairs also ask students to turn in a proposal to their teacher or school before starting their experiment.

Be sure to check with your teacher to make sure your proposal includes all the parts your school requires. This helps you get feedback, make improvements, and get permission to begin your experiment.

What You'll Do on the Next Pages:
- Write your project title, question, and hypothesis
- Explain why your project matters
- List your materials and steps
- Identify your variables
- Plan how you'll collect your data safely and fairly

When your proposal is complete, ask your teacher or adult to review and sign it.

Once your plan is approved, you'll be ready to start your investigation in the next section: The Experiment!

🐾 Cat Tip: "Planning, testing, and sharing — that's how scientists think and work!"

Brainstorm Your Ideas

Every science project starts with curiosity!
What are you interested in learning more about? What do you notice
in the world around you that makes you wonder "Why?" or "What if?"

Use this page to list all your ideas — even the silly or wild ones.
Scientists often think of many questions before choosing one to test.

Think About:

- Things you notice in nature (plants, weather, animals)
- How objects work (bridges, magnets, batteries)
- Everyday mysteries (melting, floating, glowing, or growing)
- Science topics you've learned about in school or read in a book

My Ideas:

1. _____

_____

2. _____

_____

3. _____

_____

4. _____

_____

5. _____

_____

Now Ask Yourself:

- Can I measure or test this idea?
- Do I have the materials and time to do it safely?
- Will it make a fun and fair experiment?

Sketch Your Science Ideas

Take time to sketch some of your ideas. Scientists and inventors often draw their thoughts to see how something might work in real life. Use this page to draw and label two or three different science ideas. Your sketches don't have to be perfect. They're just a way to think through what you could test or build.

Choosing Your Final Question

Now that you've brainstormed lots of ideas, it's time to choose the one you'll turn into your science fair project. Scientists pick questions that are clear, specific, and can be tested through observation or an experiment.

Look back at your brainstorm list and circle two or three that you like best. Then think about which one is the most doable, safe, and interesting to you.

Questions to Ask Yourself:

- Can I test this idea with materials I can find at home or school?
- Can I measure or observe the results easily?
- Will this project help me learn something new or solve a problem?
- Can I complete it safely and on time?

Write your top ideas below, then choose your final question!

My Top Ideas	What Makes It a Good Question?

My Final Science Question:

_____

_____

_____

_____

Hypothesis

A hypothesis is your best guess about what will happen in your experiment.

It is based on what you already know and what you expect to observe.

A good hypothesis is:
- A clear prediction
- Something you can test
- Often written as an "If..., then..." statement

Examples:
- If plants get more sunlight, then they will grow taller.
- If I use different bridge designs, then the truss bridge will hold the most weight.
- If I water one plant more often than another, then the one with more water will grow faster.

Now write your hypothesis below:

_____

_____

_____

_____

Why I Think This:

_____

_____

_____

_____

Use what you already know to explain your prediction.

🐾 Blue Explains: "A hypothesis is just a prediction — it's okay if it turns out to be wrong. That's still good science!"

Identify Your Variables

Every experiment has variables — things that can change or be measured.
Understanding your variables helps you design a fair test and collect clear data.

There are three main types of variables in a science experiment:

Type of Variable	What It Means	Example
Independent Variable	What you change on purpose in your experiment.	The amount of sunlight each plant gets.
Dependent Variable	What you measure or observe to see what happens.	The height of each plant after one week.
Controlled Variables	The things you keep the same to make it a fair test.	Same type of plant, same soil, same pot, same amount of water.

Now try it with your experiment:
Independent Variable (what you change):

_____

Dependent Variable (what you measure):

_____

Controlled Variables (what you keep the same):

_____

🐾 Adeline's Tip: "Independent begins with I, so it is the one I changed"

Making a Fair Test

A fair test means changing only one thing at a time while keeping everything else the same. This helps you know for sure what caused your results.

Scientists design fair tests so that their experiments are accurate, repeatable, and trustworthy.

To make your experiment fair:
- Change only one variable (the independent variable).
- Measure only one outcome (the dependent variable).
- Keep everything else the same (the controlled variables).
- Record your data carefully and honestly.
- Repeat your test more than once to make sure your results are consistent.

Example:

A student wants to find out how light affects plant growth.
The independent variable is the amount of light each plant receives.
The dependent variable is how tall each plant grows.
The controlled variables are the soil type, water amount, pot size, and kind of plant.
By changing only the light and keeping everything else the same, the test is fair.

My Fair Test Checklist:
☐ I am changing only one thing in my experiment.
☐ I am measuring one main result.
☐ I am keeping everything else the same.
☐ I will repeat my experiment more than once.

🐾 Adeline's Tip: "Fair tests help scientists trust their results."

Materials & Procedure

Every good experiment has a clear plan. Before you start testing, write down what you'll need and what steps you'll take. This helps you stay organized and makes it easier for someone else to repeat your experiment.

Materials:
List everything you will use. Include tools, measuring instruments, and any special materials or ingredients.

☐ _____ ☐ _____ ☐ _____
☐ _____ ☐ _____ ☐ _____
☐ _____ ☐ _____ ☐ _____

☐ _____ ☐ _____ ☐ _____
☐ _____ ☐ _____ ☐ _____
☐ _____ ☐ _____ ☐ _____

A good scientist writes down each step so that someone else could repeat the experiment and get the same results. Write your steps in order, using short, clear sentences.

Tip from Oreo 🐾: "Simple steps are easier to follow. Imagine you are giving directions to a friend."

1. _____
2. _____
3. _____
4. _____
5. _____
6. _____
7. _____
8. _____
9. _____
10. _____

Design Your Experiment!

Before you write your official proposal, use this page to sketch out your plan.
Think of it like a blueprint for your science fair project.

Sketch Your Setup

Draw what your experiment will look like.
Include your model, tools, and anything you will need.

Key Ideas to Think About

- What question am I testing?
- What do I think will happen?
- What materials will I need?
- How will I measure or compare my results?
- How many tests or trials will I run?
- Do I need to build or set up anything ahead of time?

🐾 Blue says: "Sketch it first! It helps you see your experiment before you build it."
🐾 Oreo adds: "And you can always erase and try again!"

Pulling It All Together

You've learned how scientists plan and test ideas, written your question, made a hypothesis, listed your materials, and organized your steps.

Now it's time to pull everything together into one complete plan — your science fair proposal!

Your proposal is like a map for your experiment. It shows what you plan to test, what you think will happen, and how you'll make sure your test is fair.

Most school science fairs ask students to turn in a proposal to their teacher before they start their experiment.

This helps make sure your plan is safe, clear, and ready to go.

Before You Write Your Proposal:
□ I have a clear science question
□ I wrote my hypothesis and why I think it's true
□ I identified my variables
□ I made a list of materials I'll need
□ I wrote my step-by-step procedure
□ I thought about safety rules to follow
□ I checked with my teacher to make sure I have every needed to turn in

When you've checked all the boxes, you're ready to write your Science Fair Project Proposal on the next page.

🐾 Cat Tip: "Check your teacher to see if they require any extra parts before turning it in for approval!"

My Science Fair Project Proposal

Project Title: _____

Student Name: _____

Date: _____

A. Rationale

B. Research Question, Hypothesis, and Expected Outcome

Research Question:

Hypothesis:

Expected Outcome:

C. Variables

Independent Variable (What I will change)

Dependent Variable (What I will measure)

Controlled Variables (What will stay the same)

D. Project Plan

Materials

☐ _____ ☐ _____ ☐ _____

☐ _____ ☐ _____ ☐ _____

☐ _____ ☐ _____ ☐ _____

☐ _____ ☐ _____ ☐ _____

Procedures

1. _____
2. _____
3. _____
4. _____
5. _____
6. _____
7. _____
8. _____
9. _____
10. _____

E. Risk and Safety

☐ Ask an adult for help with tools or hot water.
☐ Clean up any spills right away.
☐ Keep electronics away from water.
☐ Wear goggles if needed.
☐ Other: _____
☐ Other: _____

F. Data Collection and Analysis

☐ Use a table or chart.
☐ Repeat each test three times.
☐ Take photos or draw pictures.
☐ Make a graph to show results.
☐ Write a short conclusion.
☐ Other: _____
☐ Other: _____

G. Bibliography or Research Sources

(List any books, videos, or websites you used for ideas.)

YOUR EXPERIMENT: TEST, MEASURE, AND ANALYZE

The Experiment

Now that your plan is ready and your safety checklist is complete, it's time to start your experiment! This is the fun part — where you test your ideas and collect data to see what really happens.

Scientists follow their procedures carefully, take notes, and record their results so they can understand the evidence behind their discoveries.

Use the next few pages to write down your observations, data, and reflections. Be as detailed as possible. Remember, good scientists write enough information so someone else could repeat the experiment exactly the same way.

What You'll Do in This Section:
- Follow your procedure step by step.
- Record your data each time you test.
- Repeat your test if possible to check your results.
- Take clear notes and measurements.
- Keep everything organized and labeled.

By the end of this section, you'll have all the data and results you need for your science fair board and presentation.

Before You Begin:
- ☐ My proposal has been reviewed and approved
- ☐ I have all my materials ready to use
- ☐ I have a safe and clean workspace
- ☐ I understand each step of my procedure
- ☐ I'm ready to make careful observations and record my data

When you've checked all the boxes, you're ready to start your experiment and watch science in action!

Design Your Model

Some science fair projects include making a model or building something to test your idea.

A model can be a small version, a simple design, or a hands-on setup that shows how something works in real life.

Building your model helps you:
- Test your hypothesis in a realistic way
- Observe how systems or designs behave
- Practice engineering and problem-solving skills

Examples:
- A bridge made from straws to test which design holds the most weight
- A simple water filter made with sand and gravel to explore clean water solutions
- A paper airplane design to test how wing shape affects flight distance

Plan Before You Build:

What will your model show or test? _____

_____

What materials will you use?_____

_____

What steps will you take to build it? _____

_____

How will you test it safely and fairly?_____

_____

Sketch Your design on the next page

🐾 Adeline's Tip: "Models help us see science in action!"

🐾 Blue Adds: "Measure twice, build once — and don't glue your tail."

🐾 Oreo Says: "If it rolls, flies, or moves, I call first dibs on testing!"

Sketch Your Design Here

Use this page to draw and label your ideas. You can make notes about what each part does, what materials you'll use, or how you'll test it. If you change your design later, that's okay. Improving your model is part of the process.

Don't Forget to Take Photos and Notes!

Good scientists keep track of their work as they go.
Taking photos and writing notes helps you remember what happened
at each step of your experiment. It also makes it easier to share your
results later.

You can take photos or draw quick sketches to show what your
experiment looks like at different times. Be sure to include anything
that changes or surprises you!

Here Are Some Ideas:
- Take a photo or make a drawing before you start
- Write notes about what your setup looks like
- Record what you see while the ice is melting
- Take another photo or make a drawing after your experiment ends
- Add short captions to explain each picture or sketch

Quick Reminders:
☐ Take photos or draw pictures as your experiment changes
☐ Write notes about what you notice
☐ Include dates or times if you can
☐ Keep your notes organized so you can use them later for your
science fair board

🐾 Cat Tip: "Every great scientist keeps a record. You never know when
a small detail will lead to a big discovery!"

**Remember to keep taking
photos and notes
throughout your
experiment, not just at
the beginning or end.**

From Plan to Build

You've designed your model and thought through how it will work. Now it's time to bring your ideas to life.

Scientists and engineers don't just imagine, they create and test. Building your model helps you see whether your design works the way you expected. It's also a chance to make changes, solve problems, and improve your plan along the way.

As you get ready to build, remember:
- Double-check your materials and tools.
- Review your sketch and make sure it's clear.
- Set up a safe and organized workspace.
- Work carefully and take your time.

Build Reflection

After you finish building, take a moment to think about how it went. What worked well? What needed fixing or adjusting? How did your model change from your original plan?

What Worked Well: _____

_____

What I Changed or Improved: _____

_____

What Surprised Me: _____

_____

🐾 Adeline's Tip: "Every experiment teaches something, even when things don't go as planned."
🐾 Blue Adds: "Problem-solving is just science in action."
🐾 Oreo Says: "If you fixed it with tape, that's basically engineering."

Ready to Test

You've built your model and made your plan. Before you start testing, make sure everything is ready. Good scientists take time to prepare so they can collect accurate data and stay safe.

Use this page to double-check your setup and get organized before your experiment begins.

My Pre-Test Checklist:
- ☐ My model or setup is complete and ready to test
- ☐ All materials and tools are in place
- ☐ My data table or notebook is ready for observations
- ☐ I have a timer, measuring tools, or any other instruments I need
- ☐ My adult helper or teacher has reviewed my setup
- ☐ I've checked my safety plan and workspace
- ☐ I'm ready to start collecting data carefully and calmly

Think Ahead:
What do you expect will happen during your test?

_____

_____

What might go wrong, and how can you fix or adjust it safely?

_____

_____

🐾 Adeline's Tip: "Preparation helps your experiment run smoothly from start to finish."

🐾 Blue Adds: "Double-check everything before you begin."

🐾 Oreo Says: "And make sure no tails are in the way of the experiment!"

Test & Observe

Now that your model or setup is ready, it's time to see what happens! In this step, you will test your experiment by observing, measuring, and recording what occurs as you carry out your plan.

Scientists call this collecting data. That means making careful observations, taking measurements, and writing down what you notice over time.

Use your tools to keep track of changes, measure results, and record your notes neatly and accurately.

What You'll Do in This Step:
- Watch your experiment carefully as it takes place
- Record what you see before, during, and after each test
- Measure your results using the correct tools
- Keep your notes neat, detailed, and honest

Set Up Your Data Table

On the next page, you will make your own data table.
Before you begin, decide what information you need to record.

Follow these steps:
1. Look at your science question. What are you testing or comparing?
2. Decide what you will measure or observe during your experiment.
3. Write a clear title at the top of your table.
4. Label each column with what it will show. Example: "Time (seconds)" or "Plant Height (cm)."
5. Make sure every column includes units of measurement if needed.
6. Leave enough rows to record data for all of your tests or trials.
7. Your table should be neat, clear, and ready for collecting data.

Example:

Below is an example of how you might label your table headings for an experiment that compares two setups — such as how sunlight affects two different plants.

Day	Sunlight	Notes	Shade	Notes
1	3 CM	Leaves look green	3 CM	Leaves look green
3	6.5 CM	Stem is a little stronger	5 CM	Growth slower
10	11 CM	Very healthy	9 CM	Weak stem, fewer leaves

Title: _____

Time / Trial / Variable	Observation 1	Measurement 1 (with units)	Observation 2 (if comparing setups)	Measurement 2 (with units)

Graph It Out

You have finished collecting your data. Now it's time to organize it so others can understand what you discovered. Graphs help scientists see patterns, spot trends, and compare results quickly.

You can use your data to create different types of graphs that show what happened in your experiment.

🐾 Blue Says: "Graphs turn numbers into stories!"
🐾 Oreo Adds: "And colorful graphs catch everyone's attention!"

What You'll Do in This Step:
- Use your data table to make a graph that shows your results clearly
- Label your axes (the bottom and side lines)
- Add a descriptive title that tells what your graph shows
- Use colors or patterns to make different variables easy to see
- Look for patterns or differences in your results

Before You Begin:
□ My data table is complete and easy to read
□ I have pencils, rulers, or colors ready
□ I will label everything neatly and include units
□ I'm ready to find patterns and compare results

🐾 Cat Tip: "Neat graphs make your data shine!"

Organize & Visualize
Making Sense of Data

Key Words to Know:

<u>Data</u>: Information you collect (like how many times something happens).

<u>Bar</u>: A rectangle that shows how much of something there is.

<u>X-Axis</u>: The line across the bottom. It shows what you are measuring (like types of ice cream).

<u>Y-Axis</u>: The line going up the side. It shows how many or how much.

<u>Label</u>: A word or phrase that tells what something means.

<u>Title</u>: The name of your graph—it tells what it's about.

<u>Compare</u>: Look at how bars are the same or different.

Look Back at My Data

What did I measure or observe in my experiment?	How did I record my data? (notes, numbers, pictures)

✍️ Graph It Out - Line Graph

A line graph shows how something changes over time.
Scientists use line graphs to track progress, patterns, or changes in data such as temperature, growth, or speed.

You'll use the chart on the next page to plot your data and connect your observations into a line.

Step 1: Label the bottom (X-axis) with what changes over time (for example, Time in minutes, Days, or Trials).
Step 2: Label the side (Y-axis) with what you measured (such as Temperature (°C), Height (cm), or Speed (m/s)).
Step 3: Plot each data point carefully on the graph.
Step 4: Connect the points with straight lines to show how your data changed.
Step 5 (optional): If you are comparing two setups, draw a separate line for each one. Use different colors or dashed lines to tell them apart.

Blue and Oreo's Line Graph Example

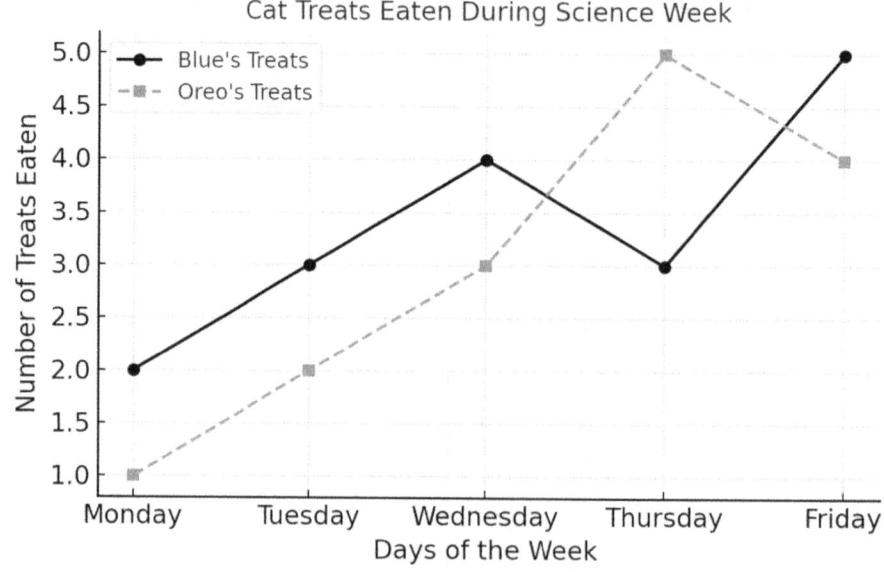

Cat Treats Eaten During Science Week

- This example shows how many treats Blue and Oreo ate each day during Science Week.
- The solid line shows Blue's treats, and the dashed line shows Oreo's treats.
- Look closely to see which cat's treat count went up or down as the week went on.

Title: _____

Y Axis: _____

X Axis: _____

 # Graph It Out - Bar Graph

Now let's look at your data another way, in a bar graph.
Bar graphs make it easy to compare results side by side and see which values are higher or lower.

Step 1: Label the bottom (X-axis) with what you are comparing (for example, Plant in Sunlight and Plant in Shade).

Step 2: Label the side (Y-axis) with what you measured (such as Height (cm), Temperature (°C), or Weight (g)).

Step 3: Draw your bars to match your data values.

Step 4: Leave equal spaces between bars and make them the same width.

Step 5 (optional): Use different colors, patterns, or shading to represent separate groups or trials.

Blue and Oreo's Bar Graph Example

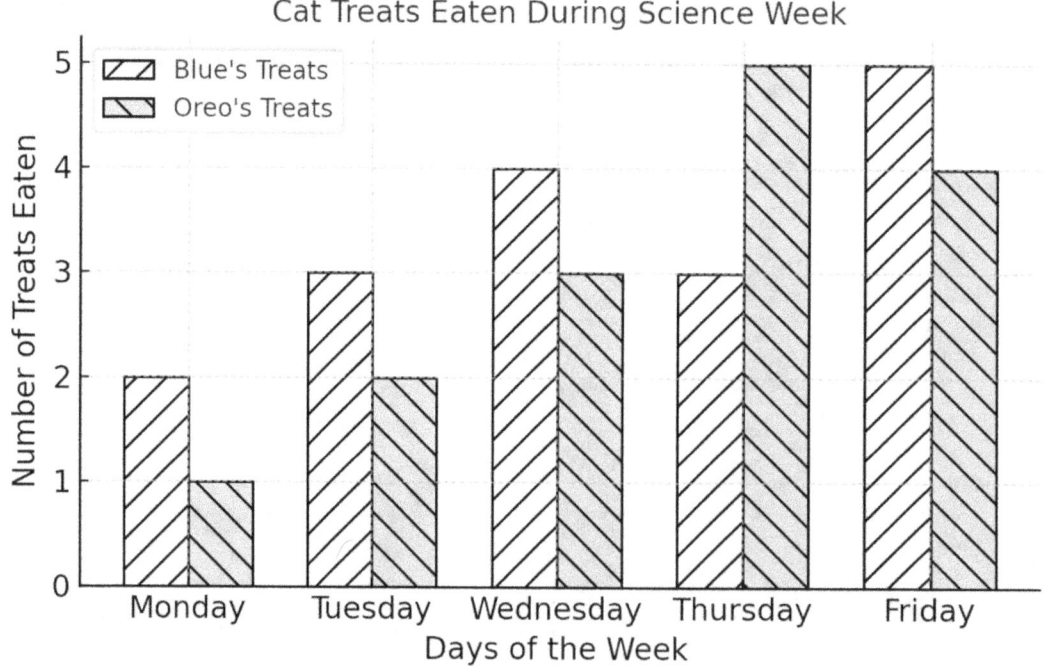

- In this example, each bar shows how many treats Blue and Oreo ate on different days of the week.
- The patterns on the bars make it easy to tell which cat ate more treats each day.

Title: _____

Y Axis: ___

X Axis: _____

Graph It Out - Pie Chart

Now let's look at the data with a pie chart!
Pie charts show how each part compares to the whole. Scientists and data analysts use them to show percentages or portions of a total amount.

Step 1: Decide what you want to show as parts of a whole (for example, types of materials tested, different outcomes, or favorite choices).
Step 2: Add up the total number of data points.
Step 3: Calculate what portion each category represents. You can use percentages or fractions.
Step 4: Draw a circle and divide it into slices. Each slice should match the size of its data portion.
Step 5: Use labels or a key to show what each slice means.

Blue and Oreo's Pie Chart Example

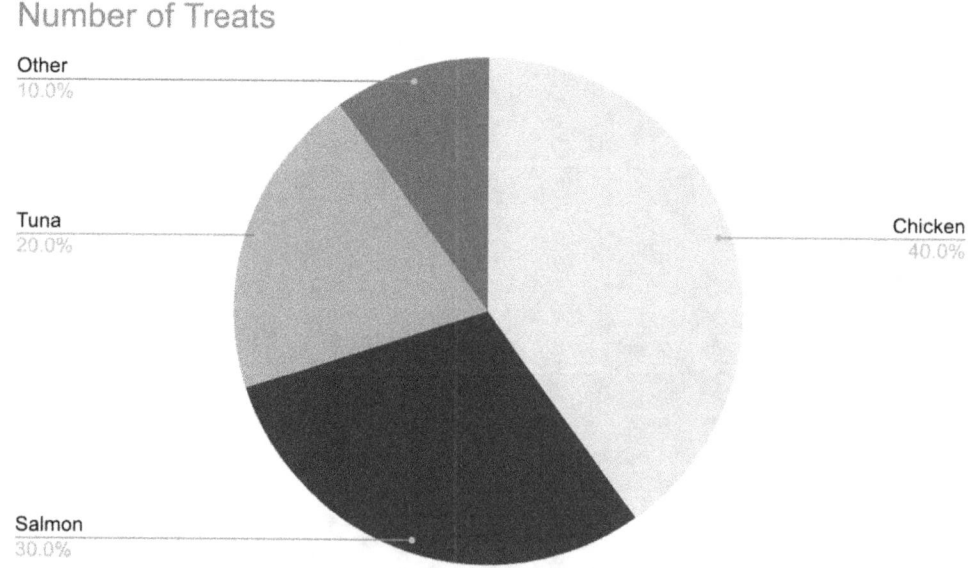

Number of Treats

Other 10.0%
Tuna 20.0%
Chicken 40.0%
Salmon 30.0%

In this example:
- Each slice shows what portion of the total treats came from that flavor.
- The larger the slice, the greater the amount.
- Labels or a color key help readers see the data clearly.

🐾 Adeline's Reminder: "Pie charts make it easy to see which category takes up the biggest slice!"

Title: _____

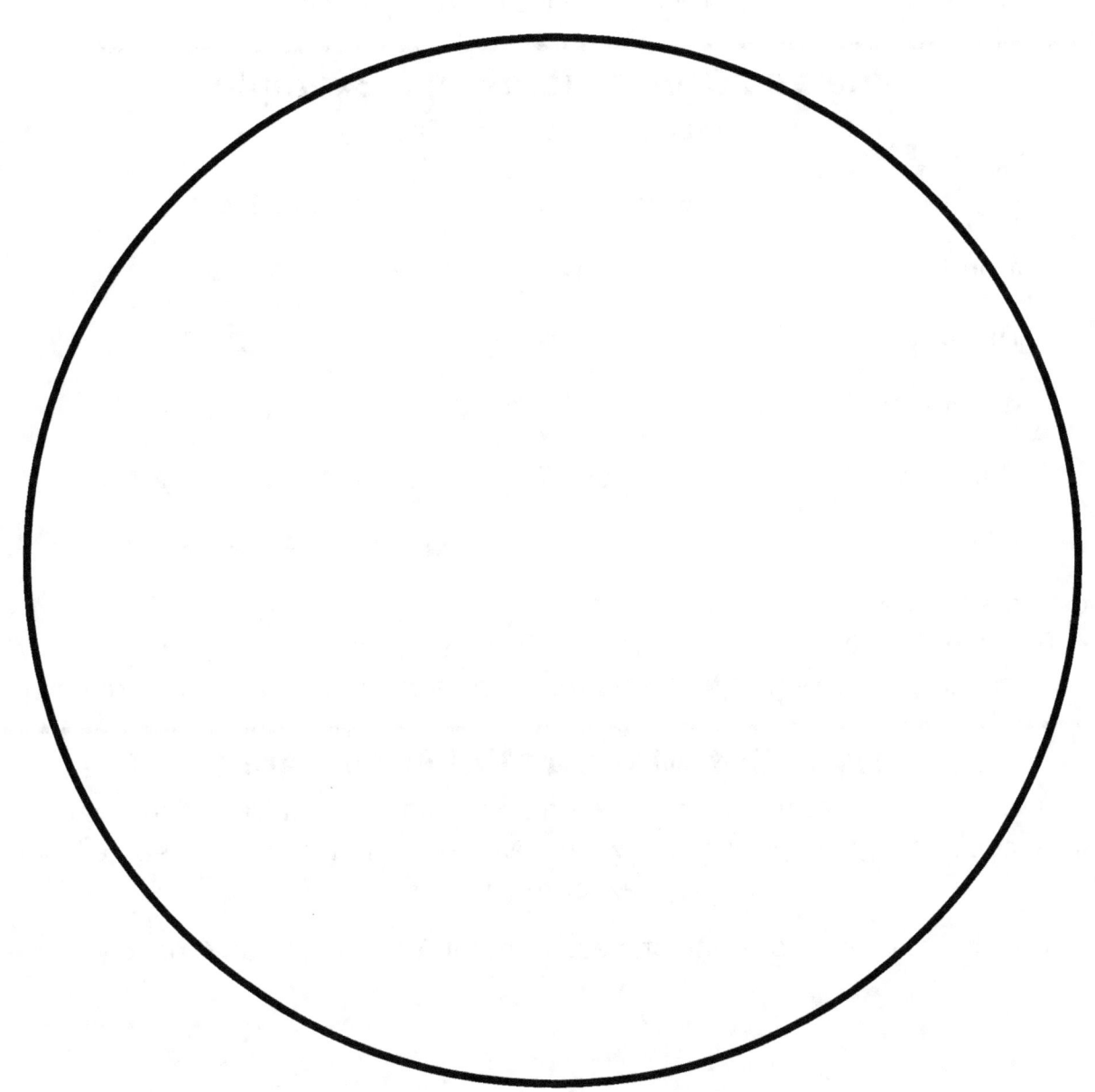

Graph It Out - Pictograph

A pictograph uses pictures or symbols to show numbers. It is another way to display your results.

Step 1: Choose Your Symbol
Step 2: Create Your Key
Step 3: Draw Your Pictograph

Blue and Oreo's Pictograph Example

Example Key: 🐾 = 1 Treat

Day	Blue's Treats	Oreo's Treats
Monday	🐾 🐾	🐾
Tuesday	🐾 🐾 🐾	🐾 🐾
Wednesday	🐾 🐾 🐾 🐾	🐾 🐾 🐾
Thursday	🐾 🐾 🐾	🐾 🐾 🐾 🐾 🐾
Friday	🐾 🐾 🐾 🐾 🐾	🐾 🐾 🐾 🐾

So across the week:
- Blue ate steadily more treats through the week, with a small dip on Thursday.
- Oreo started slower but had a big snack spike on Thursday (her record day!).

Try It Out: Make a Mini Pictograph!

Here's your chance to turn your experiment data into a quick picture chart.
Use symbols to show how much the water level rose for land ice and sea ice in your experiment.

Each symbol stands for one unit of measurement. You can use any shape you like.

Which Graph Should I Use?

What story do my graphs tell about my experiment?

Did anything surprise me when I look at my graphs?

What patterns or trends do I see?

What charts tell the story of the data the best? Which ones do I want to use on your science fair board?

Make a Chart on the Computer

Using Google Sheets

Google Sheets is a great tool for organizing data and creating charts. You can make bar, line, and pie charts to help others see your results clearly.

Part 1: Enter Your Data

1. Go to Google Sheets and open a blank spreadsheet.
2. Type your labels (like trial names or materials) in the first column.
3. Type your numbers or measurements in the next column(s).

Example: Raw Data Table

Light Color	Trial 1	Trial 2	Trial 3
Red Light	8	9	7
Blue Light	10	11	10
White Light	12	13	12

Part 2: Make Charts to Show Your Averages

Now that your data is entered, you can use the same information to make other kinds of charts that compare averages or show changes over time.

Calculate your averages.

1. Add all your trial numbers and divide by the number of tests.
   - Example: $(8 + 9 + 7) \div 3 = 8$.
2. Create a new table with your averages.

Light Color	Average
Red Light	8
Blue Light	10
White Light	12

Part 3: Show Averages with Bar, Line, or Pie Charts

1. Insert → Chart → select Bar, Line, or Pie.
2. Use your average data in the chart.
   ○ Bar Chart: Compare groups or categories.
   ○ Line Chart: Show changes or patterns over time.
   ○ Pie Chart: Show parts of a whole.
3. Add a clear title (for example: Average Plant Growth Under Different Lights).
4. Label your axes and check that your chart matches your data.
5. Save or print your finished chart for your project.

Example Bar Chart Made in Google Sheets

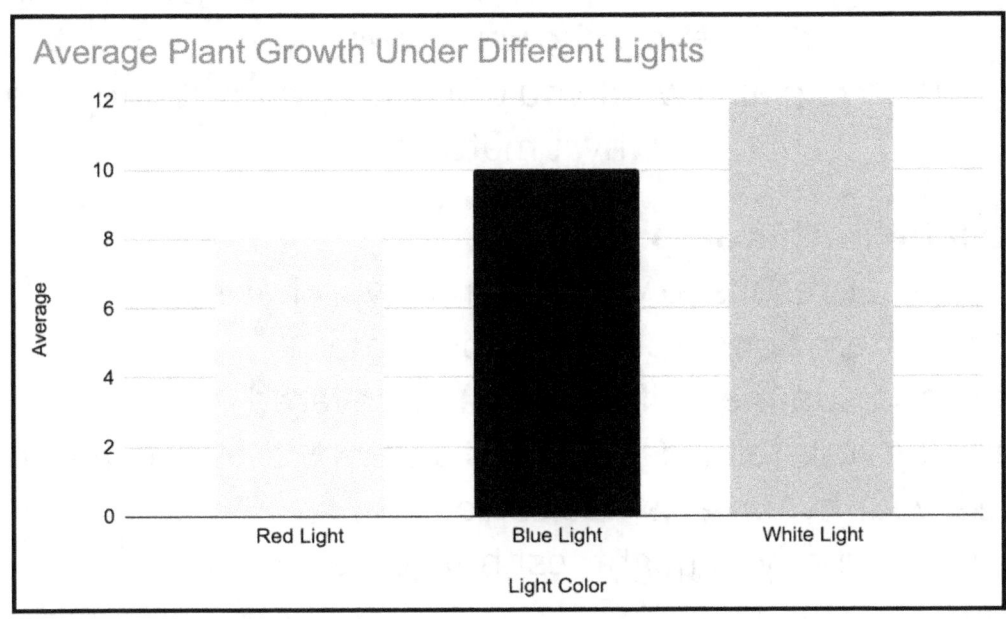

Part 4: Add Your Chart to Your Report or Slides

When your chart is ready, you can add it to your science fair report or presentation.

1. Click the three dots (⋮) in the top-right corner of your chart.
2. Select Copy chart.
3. Open your Google Doc or Google Slides file.
4. Click Edit → Paste.
5. Choose Link to spreadsheet if you want the chart to update automatically when your data changes.

Reflect on Your Hypothesis & Conclusion

You have planned, tested, observed, and recorded your results. Now it is time to look back and think about what you learned.

Scientists always reflect on their work to see how their results compare to their original ideas. This helps them understand what their data means and what questions they might ask next.

In this section, you will review your hypothesis, study your graphs and data, and write your conclusion.
Your conclusion explains what you discovered, why it happened, and why it matters.

What You'll Do in This Step:
- Compare your results to your original hypothesis
- Look for patterns or surprises in your data
- Write a short summary of what you discovered
- Explain why your results happened and why they are important
- Decide if your hypothesis was correct
- Think about what you might test next time

Before You Begin:
☐ I have finished all my data tables and graphs
☐ I remember what my hypothesis was
☐ I understand what my results show
☐ I can explain how my data answers my question
☐ I am ready to write what I learned clearly and neatly

🐾 Cat Tip: "Even if your guess was wrong, you still made a great discovery!"

Reflect on Your Hypothesis

Think back to your original question or hypothesis.

🖊 Was your hypothesis correct? Why or why not?

🖊 What did you learn from your results?

✍ My Results

What did I discover from my experiment?
Write your results here:

_____
_____
_____
_____
_____

☐ My hypothesis was correct
☐ My hypothesis was not correct
☐ My results were different than I expected

My Conclusion

A conclusion explains what you learned and why it matters.

Sentence starters to help you:

The results show that _____

_____

_____

_____

_____

This happened because _____

_____

_____

_____

_____

This is important because _____

_____

_____

_____

_____

Write your conclusion here:

_____

_____

_____

_____

Reflection

Every scientist thinks about what went well and what could be better.

One thing I would do differently is:

_____

_____

_____

_____

_____

One new question I have is:

_____

_____

_____

_____

_____

What would you test next if you had more time, materials, or tools?:

_____

_____

_____

_____

_____

One thing I am proud of is:

_____

_____

_____

_____

_____

Real-World Connection

Science doesn't stop at the lab table. It connects to everything around us!
Now that you've finished your experiment, think about how your findings matter in the real world.

Scientific discoveries help people make better choices, design new technology, protect the environment, and improve everyday life. Even small classroom experiments can help us understand big ideas about how the world works.

My Thoughts

_____
_____
_____
_____
_____

How does my experiment connect to the world around me?

_____
_____
_____
_____

Why is it important to understand what I tested in this experiment?

_____
_____
_____
_____

Choose Your Connection

Science connects to the world in many different ways.
Pick the topic area that fits your experiment best and answer the questions below.

Environmental Science
(Examples: water, energy, pollution, climate, recycling)

- How could this experiment help people take better care of the environment?
- What might happen if people ignored this science in real life?
- How could what I learned be used to protect animals, plants, or natural resources?

Engineering and Design
(Examples: bridges, circuits, inventions, structures, simple machines)

- How could engineers use what I learned to make something stronger or safer?
- How does this experiment show problem-solving in action?
- What real-world challenge could my design or idea help improve?

Life Science and Health
(Examples: plants, ecosystems, nutrition, exercise, germs)

- How does this experiment help us understand living things or healthy choices?
- What might this experiment teach farmers, doctors, or scientists?
- How could my findings help people or animals in everyday life?

What's Next? Future Research

Scientists are always asking new questions. Even after an experiment is finished, there's always more to explore! That's why science fair projects usually end with a "Future Research" section. This shows what you might test if you had more time, more tools, or a bigger lab.

Tips for Future Research

- Think bigger: What could you test with more time or better equipment?
- Add a twist: What's one change you'd try next time?
- Follow your curiosity: Did your results make you wonder about something new?

Example

Next time, I would test how different temperatures affect the speed of melting. I could also measure what happens if I use saltwater instead of freshwater to see if the results change.

Activity: Imagine Your Next Step

Fill in the blanks to dream up your future research idea!
One thing I would test next time is:

_____

Something I would change or add is:

_____

A new question I now have is:

_____

My Future Research Statement

_____
_____
_____
_____

SHARING YOUR WORK: PROJECT BOARD

Time to Share Your Project!

Time to Share Your Project!

You planned your question, did your experiment, and wrote your results. Now it is time to show off what you learned. Scientists share their discoveries with others, and your science fair board is your way of doing that.

<u>You already did most of this when you worked through your experiment!</u> You planned your question, carried out your test, and wrote down your results. Now it is time to show off what you learned. Scientists share their discoveries with others, and your science fair board is your way of doing that.

Your board should:
- Be neat, colorful, and easy to read.
- Include charts, graphs, and pictures when possible.
- Explain your project step by step so that anyone can understand it.

On the next pages, you will find:
- Descriptions of each section of the science fair board
- Steps to help you pull your work together
- Tips for organizing your board
- A plan to get ready for your presentation

Remember: Your board tells your science story!

Building Your Science Fair Board

Every science fair board is made up of different sections. Each section has a special job because it helps explain one part of your project. Below you'll find short descriptions of the main sections. You will use these to organize your own board.

Don't Forget the Cat Clues!

As you get your board ready, remember that the parts below, like your question, procedure, or results, were already completed earlier in this book. Look for the cat symbol 🐱

In the previous sections, those activities are your ready-made pieces to add to your board. No need to start from scratch. Just gather what you've already done and put it all together!

Section	What It Includes	
Title	The name of your project — make it short, clear, and catchy!	🐱
Question or Hypothesis	What you wanted to find out or what you thought would happen.	🐱
Materials	Everything you used in your experiment.	🐱
Procedure	The steps you followed.	🐱
Variables	What you changed, measured, and kept the same.	🐱
Data & Observations	Charts, drawings, or graphs that show what happened.	🐱
Results	A short summary of what you discovered.	🐱
Conclusion	What you learned and why it matters.	🐱
Real-World Connection	How your project relates to our planet and everyday life.	🐱
Future Research	What you'd test next if you could keep going.	🐱

Make Your Title Stand Out!

Your title is the first thing people will see on your science fair board. A great title should make someone curious and excited to learn more about your project. Think of it like the cover of a book. It grabs attention and gives a clue about what's inside.

Tips for Writing a Good Title

- Be clear: Make sure your title tells what the project is about.
- Be catchy: Use fun or clever words that make people want to read more.
- Keep it short: 3–8 words is usually perfect.
- Show the science: Use words that connect to your experiment.

Examples

Instead of: "Plants and Light"
Try: "Sunlight Showdown: Which Light Helps Plants Grow Best?"

Instead of: "Bridge Strength"
Try: "Bridge Battle: Which Design Holds the Most Weight?"

Instead of: "Magnets"
Try: "Magnet Power: What Pulls Strongest?"

Activity

Write 2–3 different titles for your project. Check the one you like best!

☐ Title Option 1: _____
☐ Title Option 2: _____
☐ Title Option 3: _____

🐾 Adeline says: "A great title makes people stop and say, 'Ooh, what's that about?'"

🐾 Blue adds: "Be creative but clear. Your title should tell the story of your science."

🐾 Oreo reminds you: "And make it catchy enough to get the judges' attention!"

Write a Great Introduction

Your introduction is the "welcome sign" for your science fair board. It gives people a quick background and tells them why your project is important. A good introduction makes readers curious and excited to learn more!

Tips for Writing an Introduction

- Start with a hook: Grab attention with an interesting fact or question.
- Explain the science idea: Tell what your project is about in simple words.
- Say why it matters: Connect your project to the real world.

Example (Land Ice vs. Sea Ice)

Did you know that when glaciers melt on land, they can raise sea levels all over the world? I wanted to test the difference between melting land ice and melting sea ice. My experiment shows why the kind of ice that melts really matters.

Activity: Write Your Own!

Fill in the blanks to build your introduction:

1. Start with a fun fact or question:

_____

2. Explain what your project is about:

_____

3. Say why it matters or why you wanted to test it:

_____

Now put it all together into a short introduction (3–5 sentences).

_____

_____

_____

 Show It with Visuals

Pictures, charts, and drawings help people understand your project at a glance. Visuals make your board exciting and easy to follow, even if someone only looks for a minute. Think of them as your project's story told in pictures.

Tips for Great Visuals

- Choose carefully: Add photos, charts, or drawings that really show your experiment.
- Make it clear: Label each picture so people know what they're seeing.
- Keep it neat: Glue straight, use color wisely, and avoid clutter.
- Explain with captions: A short sentence can make a picture 10x more powerful!

Examples

- A photo of your experiment setup or materials in action
- A chart showing how your results changed over time
- A drawing or diagram explaining your design or process
- A creative illustration or 3D model that helps explain your science idea

🖊 Activity: Plan Your Visuals

Check off the visuals you will include:

☐ Photos of my experiment
☐ A chart or graph of my data
☐ A drawing or diagram
☐ Something creative (cartoon, 3D model, or cutout)

🐾 Cat Tip: If your visuals make someone say "Ohhh, now I get it!", you've done a purr-fect job.

✍️ Writing Good Captions

Captions are short sentences that explain your pictures, charts, or drawings. They help people understand your project even if you aren't standing there to explain it. A good caption tells what is happening in the picture and why it's important.

Tips for captions:
- Keep them short and clear (1–2 sentences).
- Use words like "This shows…" or "Here you can see…".
- Explain the science idea, not just what's in the photo.

Example: Instead of: "My Plants", write: "This photo shows two plants grown under different light conditions. The plant in sunlight grew taller and healthier."

_____
_____
_____
_____
_____

_____
_____
_____
_____
_____

_____
_____
_____
_____

Plan My Display

Imagine your board like a puzzle. Each piece fits in a special place.
Top Center: Your title and your name.
Left Side: Your question, hypothesis, materials, and procedure.
Middle: Your data, charts, and visuals.
Right Side: Your results, conclusion, and real-world connection.

Draw a line from the words to the blank board below where the sections you should include in your science fair belong.

Title
Introduction
Question or Hypothesis
Materials
Procedures
Variable
Data (graph or chart)
Pictures, drawings, or diagrams
Results
Real-World Connection
Future Questions
Conclusion

Double-check your layout. Did you place each section of your project in the correct spot on your board?

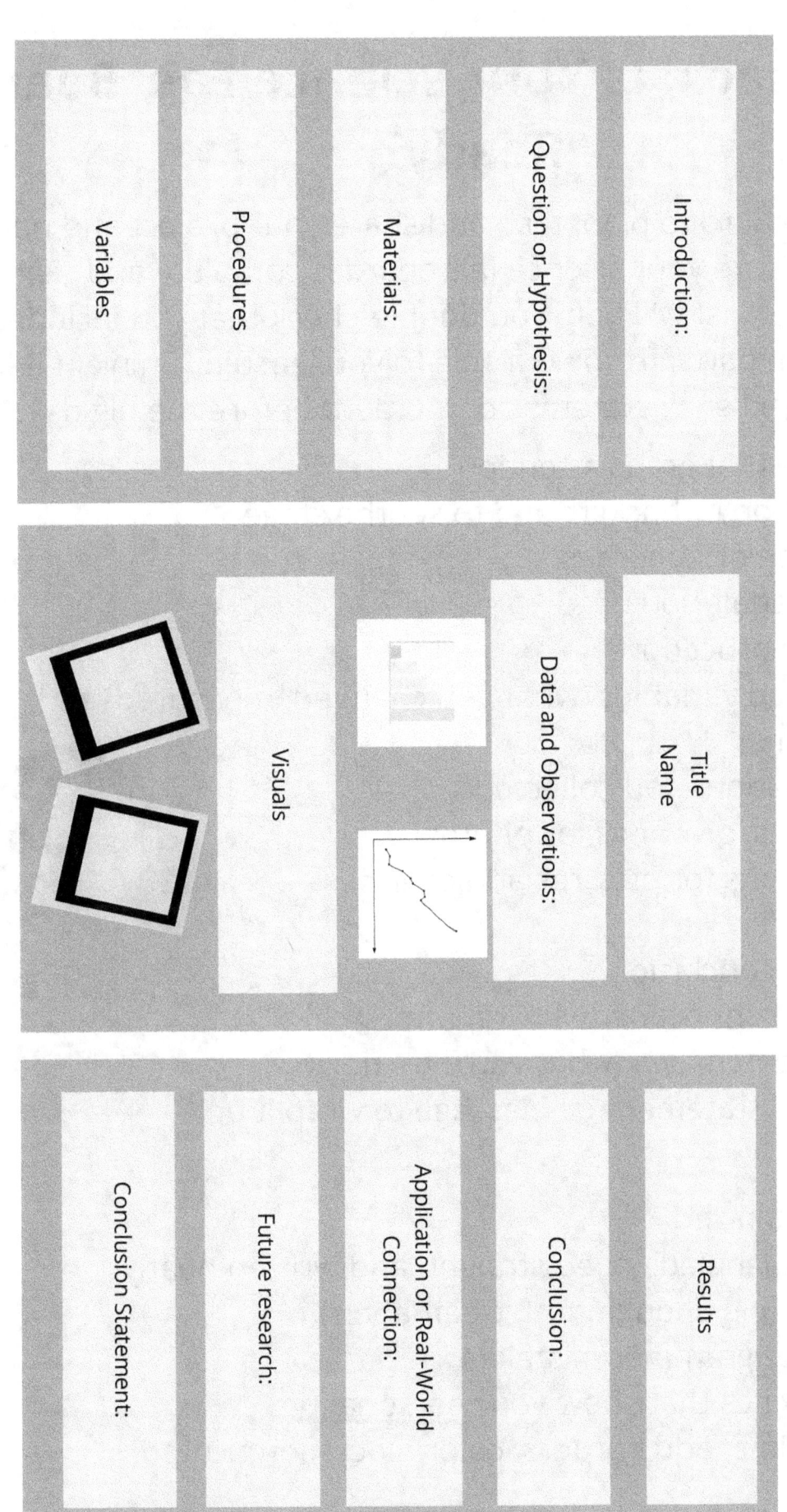

Final Check: Is Your Science Fair Board Ready?

You've worked hard to plan, test, and share your project and now it's time to make sure your science fair board is complete and ready to shine! This checklist will help you double-check that you included all the important parts, from your title to your results. Think of it like your project's "all systems go" moment before the big day.

- ☐ A catchy title that grabs attention
- ☐ An introduction or background to set the stage
- ☐ Your question or hypothesis
- ☐ A list of materials you used
- ☐ Step-by-step procedure
- ☐ Clearly labeled variables (what you changed, measured, and kept the same)
- ☐ Data/observations you collected
- ☐ Visuals (charts, drawings, or photos)
- ☐ Helpful captions for pictures and charts
- ☐ Your results
- ☐ A thoughtful conclusion
- ☐ A real-world connection (why it matters)
- ☐ A future research idea (what you'd try next)
- ☐ A strong final statement or message to wrap it up

Sparkle Check
- ☐ Neat and organized
- ☐ Everything is labeled, glued straight, and written neatly
- ☐ Easy to read (big enough font, clear labels)
- ☐ No spelling or grammar mistakes
- ☐ Creative touches that show your personality
- ☐ If you have time, add borders, color blocks, or printed captions

Adeline's Pro Tips

Getting my science fair board ready was a big job, but I found a few tricks that made it easier (and more fun!). Here are my best tips to help your board shine:

Plan your layout and check for mistakes.
Before you glue or tape anything, place all your pieces on the board to see how they fit. Move things around until it looks just right. Read your writing out loud or ask someone to help you check for spelling and grammar before you print. I definitely had some mistakes I needed to fix before glueing down.

Type it up.
I had a LOT of writing, so I used the computer to type most of my text. It looked neater, was easier to read, and saved space on the board. It also helped with the mistakes I mentioned earlier.

Make a model to show off.
Build or display something from your project like a model, a simple demo, or a photo series. It helps people see your experiment in action and gives you something to talk about during the fair.

Go bigger if you can.
My first year, I picked a smaller board, and it was hard to fit in all the parts. Now I definitely get a bigger one so my visuals and writing have room to breathe.

Bonus Cat Caution: "Watch out for cat fur! Oreo tried to "help me" once, and I spent half an hour picking fur off my board. Keep your helpers at a safe distance when you're gluing or taping."

SHARING YOUR WORK: PRESENTING AT THE SCIENCE FAIR

Presenting at the Science Fair

You've done the hard work, and now it's time to share it! Presenting at the science fair is your chance to show off everything you've discovered. It's not just about the board; it's about you telling your science story with confidence and excitement.

When judges, teachers, friends, or families stop by your project, they want to hear:
- **What you tested** and why it matters
- **What you found out** from your experiment
- **What surprised you** or made you curious
- **What you might test** next

Remember: You are the expert on your project. No one else knows it better than you!

Presentation Mindset

Think of it like being a teacher or storyteller. Your job is to help people understand your project and why it's awesome.

🐾 Cat Tip: If Blue and Oreo were in the audience, they'd want you to explain it clearly and with excitement, like you're telling them your favorite story.

? Questions Judges Might Ask ?

When judges visit your project, they want to hear YOUR science story.   Here are some common questions they might ask. Practice answering them so you feel ready!

About Your Project

- What is your project about?
- Why did you choose this topic?
- What was your science question or hypothesis?

About Your Experiment

- What materials did you use?
- What did you keep the same (controlled variables)?
- What did you change (independent variable)?
- What did you measure (dependent variable)?

About Your Results

- What did you observe?
- What did your data show?
- Was your hypothesis correct? Why or why not?
- Did anything surprise you?

About the Real World

- Why does this experiment matter?
- How could people use what you learned?
- What would you test next time?

🐾 Cat Tip: "Judges aren't trying to trick you. They just want to learn from you. Smile, take your time, and explain it like you're telling a story!"

Tell Your Story - Communicating Science

My Science Story

Let's turn your project into a story that others can understand and enjoy!
Cut along the dotted lines. Write your answers on each card, then practice
using them to tell your science story!

My name is _____, and my project is called:	I chose this topic because:
My question or hypothesis was:	To test it, I used these materials:
Here's what I did (procedure):	This is what I observed or discovered:
My conclusion was:	One thing I might try next time:

Tip: Keep these answers on notecards can help you practice and remember!

INTENTIONALLY LEFT BLANK

Rehearse Your Presentation

Practice sharing your science story out loud.

Use these tips to feel calm and confident on science fair day:

✓ Stand tall and smile. You're the expert on your project!

✓ Speak clearly and make eye contact.

✓ Use your board to help explain your experiment.

✓ Point to graphs or photos when you talk about them.

✓ Thank people for stopping by your display.

Use the sentence starters below if needed:

"My name is _____, and my project is about…"

"I wanted to find out…"

"First, I…"

"Then I observed…"

"I discovered that…"

"This project helped me learn…"

"The most important thing I want my audience to remember is…"

_____

_____

_____

Circle the face that shows how you feel about sharing your project:

🐾 Questions Cats Might Ask

Blue and Oreo are very curious cats! If they were the judges at your science fair, here are the silly questions they might ask. Practice answering them too. You'll get really good at explaining your project in simple, fun ways!

Blue's Questions

- If I draw paw prints instead of numbers on the graph, is that still data?
- If I hide your materials under the couch, will that change your variables?
- If I knock over your water cup, does that count as an experiment?
- Why didn't you test if things work better when I sit on them?

Oreo's Questions

- If I fall asleep on your data table, will your results change?
- If I push your experiment off the table, does gravity count as part of your project?
- Could your experiment explain why my water bowl is always empty?
- If I lick your model, does that count as data collection?

Activity

Pick your favorite silly cat question and try to give it a serious science answer!

Example:
Cat Question: "If I knock over your cup, does that count as an experiment?"

Science Answer: "No, that would be an accident, not a real experiment. Scientists plan their tests carefully and only change one variable at a time. Knocking something over might cause new observations, but it wouldn't be a fair or controlled test."

A Little Boost Before You Present

You've worked so hard. You asked a question, ran an experiment, collected data, and discovered something new.
That makes you a real scientist!

Standing in front of your project might feel a little scary, but remember this:
You know your project better than anyone else.

You did the work, you made the observations, and you learned the lessons.
That means you already have everything you need to shine.

Here's Your Scientist Pep Talk
Be curious, not nervous. People are here to learn from you!
Speak with confidence. Your ideas matter.
Share with enthusiasm. Excitement is contagious!

Remember, even professional scientists get butterflies before they present.
You've Got This!

Now take a deep breath, look at your board, and remember this is your moment to share what you've discovered.
Shine bright, Junior Scientist. You've earned it!

My Science Fair Memories

Think back to everything you did during your science fair project.
Use this page to remember your favorite moments!

My favorite part of my project was:

The hardest part for me was:

Something I learned about myself is:

Someone who helped me was:

One thing I would try next time is:

🐾 Cat Tip: Every scientist learns and grows with each experiment.
Your next idea might be your best one yet!

Scientist

Certificate of Achievement

I, _____, completed my
very own science fair project!

I explored a big idea, tested a question, and
shared my discoveries like a real scientist.

My project title:

_____

Signed: _____ (your name!)

Date: _____

Thank Your Helpers!

Every scientist has people who cheer them on.
Your science fair project was your hard work, but you did not do it alone.
Take a moment to thank the people who supported, encouraged, and inspired you.

Use this page to write short thank-you notes. Then cut them out and give them to the people who helped you during your project.

Someone who helped me learn:

Someone who encouraged me:

Someone who inspired me:

Someone I want to thank just because:

🐾 Blue says: A good thank-you makes someone's day.
🐾 Oreo adds: If they helped your science, you can help their smile.

The Purr-Fect Science Fair Series

Discover the Purr-fect Blend of Curiosity, Cats, and Science!
Join Adeline and her two clever cats, Blue and Oreo, as they turn everyday questions into exciting science fair adventures. From powering a light with a lemon battery to comparing land ice and sea ice, each story mixes laugh-out-loud moments with real scientific inquiry that young readers can replicate at home or school.

What makes the series special?

- **Standards aligned learning:** Every title is written with the Next Generation Science Standards (NGSS) and supporting Common Core literacy skills in mind, so teachers and parents can be confident the content reinforces classroom goals for grades 3–5.
- **Step-by-step project guides:** Hands-on instructions walk readers through the exact experiment featured in the story, complete with vocabulary, materials lists, data recording charts, and troubleshooting tips.
- **Science fair success tips:** Each book includes practical advice on planning a timeline, creating a display board, presenting results, and answering judges' questions—everything a budding scientist needs to shine at the fair.
- **Data-driven thinking:** Readers learn how to collect observations, analyze patterns, and draw evidence-based conclusions, building critical skills for future STEM exploration.

Packed with fun facts, lively illustrations, and plenty of cat-powered chaos, The Purr-fect Science Fair series shows kids that science is everywhere and that the best discoveries begin with a single curious "What if...?"

Keep Exploring with Bae Data Lab

Your science journey doesn't stop here!

Visit http://baedatalab.com to learn more about Bae Data Lab INC, a nonprofit organization that uses data and storytelling to make science and learning more accessible for all. Discover how our projects, research, and community programs turn data into action and inspire the next generation of curious thinkers.

Then, visit https://purrfectbooks.baedatalab.com to explore The Purr-fect Science Fair book series and find stories that blend imagination, STEM, and hands-on discovery.

From the Purr-fect Books website, you can also find a link to our Bonus Materials & STEM Activities page. It includes extra printables, experiments, and creative challenges inspired by Adeline, Blue, and Oreo.

Keep asking questions, testing ideas, and sharing what you learn. Every scientist starts with curiosity!

About the Author

Amy Bae is a data storyteller and founder of Bae Data Lab INC, a nonprofit dedicated to making STEM accessible and engaging for all children. With over two decades of experience in education and data literacy, she combines her love of data and storytelling to create playful, meaningful learning experiences.
She's also a proud mom to Adeline who inspires her work with her endless love of science, exploration, and imagination.

Acknowledgments

To Lydia and Adeline, who piloted the very first draft of this book while working on their 6th grade science fair project. Nothing tests a parent's patience, or a child's I assume, more than a science fair project. But nothing is more exciting than seeing an idea come together. There's no one else I'd rather learn alongside with.